FIVE FINGER PIANO

5

FINGER

CHRISTMAS SONGS
Made Easy

T0081615

ISBN 978-1-4950-6911-6

HAL•LEONARD®
CORPORATION
7777 W. BLUEMOUND RD. P.O. BOX 13819 MILWAUKEE, WI 53213

Visit Hal Leonard Online at
www.halleonard.com

contents

The Christmas Song
(Chestnuts Roasting on an Open Fire)

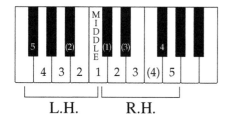

Music and Lyric by Mel Tormé
and Robert Wells

Medium slow, with expression

Chest - nuts roast - ing on an   o - pen fire,

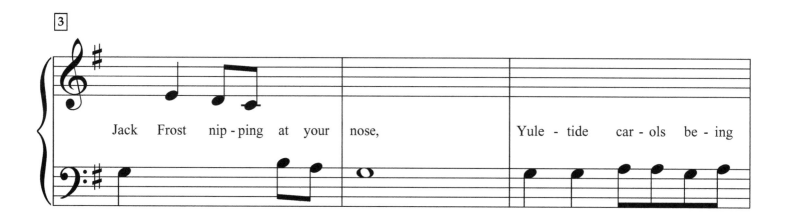

Jack Frost nip - ping at your nose,   Yule - tide car - ols be - ing

Duet Part (Student plays one octave higher than written.)

Medium slow, with expression

p
With pedal

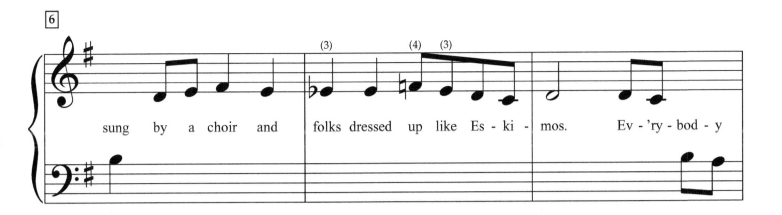

sung by a choir and folks dressed up like Es - ki - mos. Ev - 'ry - bod - y

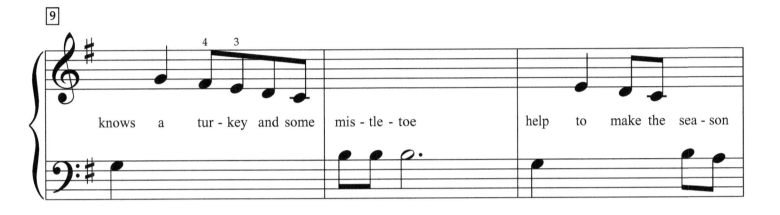

knows a tur - key and some mis - tle - toe help to make the sea - son

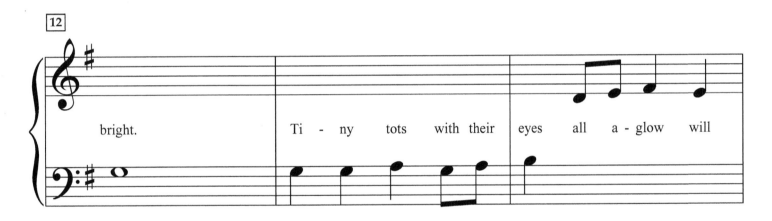

bright. Ti - ny tots with their eyes all a - glow will

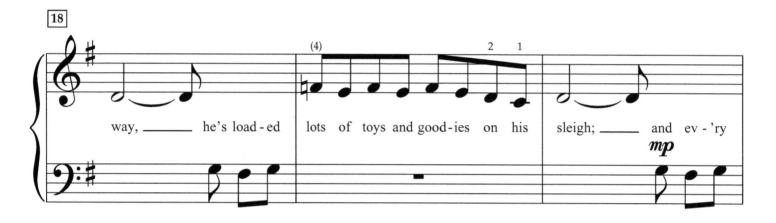

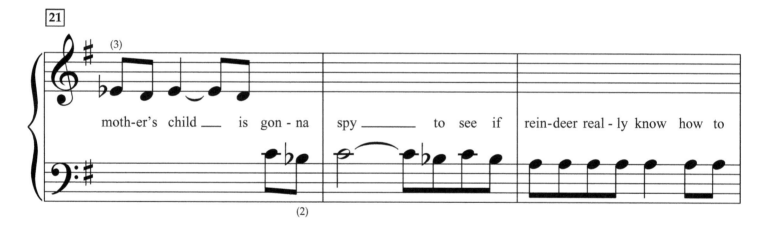

find it hard to sleep to - night. _____ They know that San - ta's on his

way, _____ he's load - ed lots of toys and good - ies on his sleigh; _____ and ev - 'ry

moth - er's child _____ is gon - na spy _____ to see if rein - deer real - ly know how to

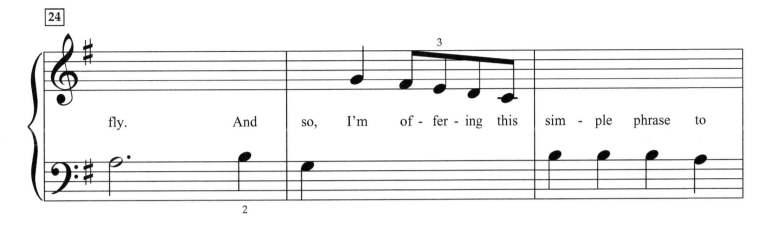

fly. And so, I'm of - fer - ing this sim - ple phrase to

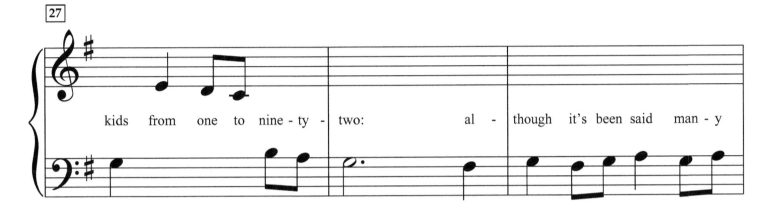

kids from one to nine - ty - two: al - though it's been said man - y

times, man - y ways, Mer - ry Christ - mas to you.

rit. *p*

rit. *pp*

Do You Want to Build a Snowman?
from FROZEN

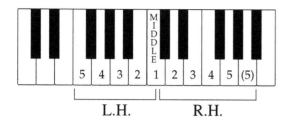

L.H.   R.H.

Music and Lyrics by Kristen Anderson-Lopez
and Robert Lopez

Moderately fast

mf Do you want to build a snow - man? _____ Come on, let's go and

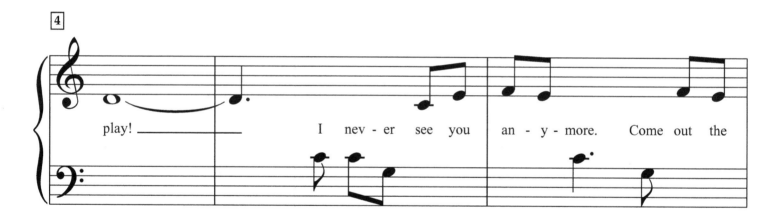

play! _____ I nev - er see you an - y - more. Come out the

Duet Part (Student plays one octave higher than written.)

Moderately fast

p

With pedal

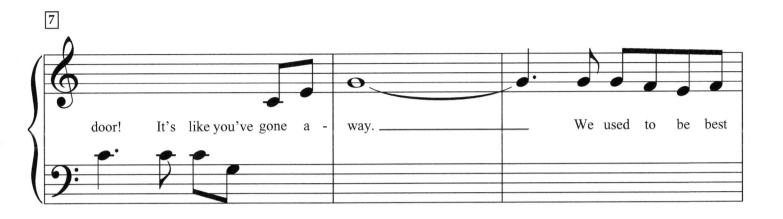

door! It's like you've gone a - way. _____ We used to be best

bud - dies.   and   now we're not. ___   I   wish you would   tell   me

why.   Do   you want   to   build   a   snow - man?

9

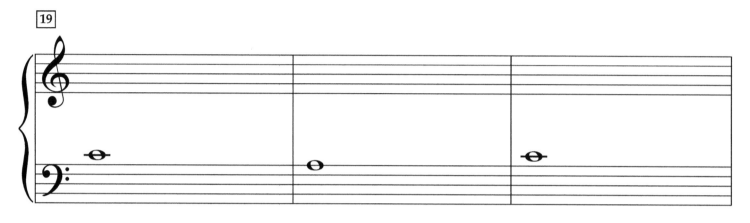

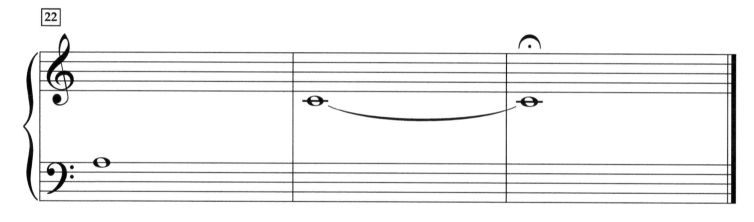

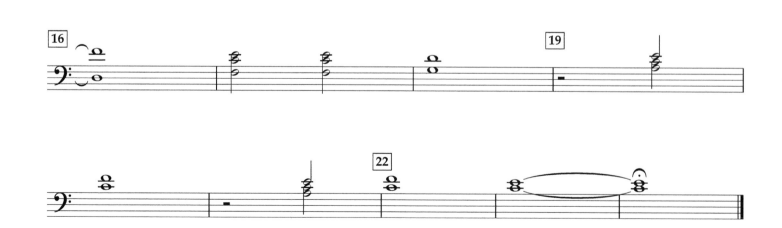

10

Let It Snow! Let It Snow! Let It Snow!

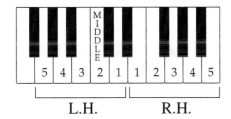

L.H.   R.H.

Words by Sammy Cahn
Music by Jule Styne

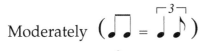

Oh, the weath-er out - side is fright - ful, but the fire is so de -

light - ful, and since we've no place to go, let it snow! Let it snow! Let it

Duet Part (Student plays one octave higher than written.)

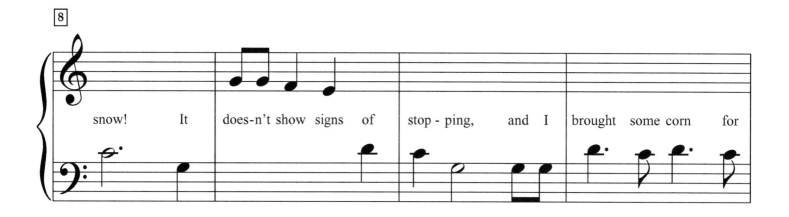

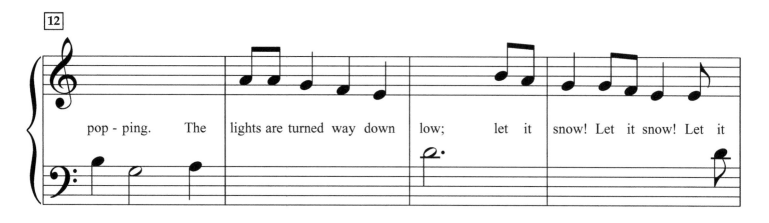

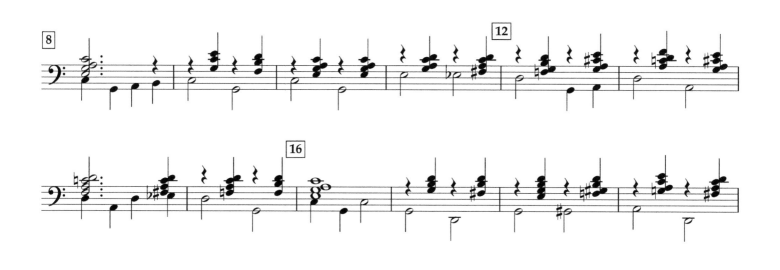

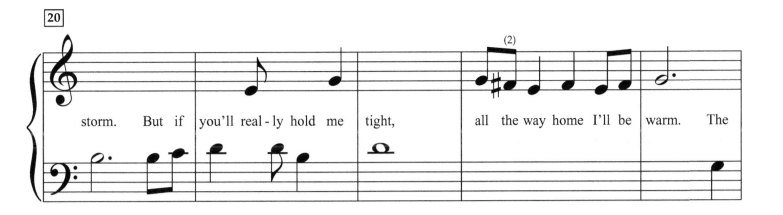

storm. But if you'll real-ly hold me tight,   all the way home I'll be warm. The

fire is slow-ly dy-ing, and my dear, we're still good-bye-ing, but as

long as you love me so, let it snow! Let it snow! Let it snow!

Have Yourself a Merry Little Christmas

from MEET ME IN ST. LOUIS

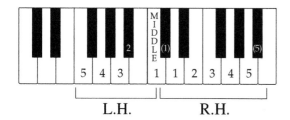

Words and Music by Hugh Martin
and Ralph Blane

Moderately slow

Have your-self a mer-ry lit-tle Christ-mas, let your heart be

light. From now on our trou-bles will be out of

Duet Part (Student plays one octave higher than written.)

Moderately slow

With pedal

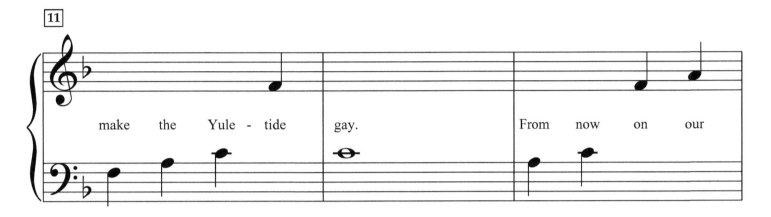

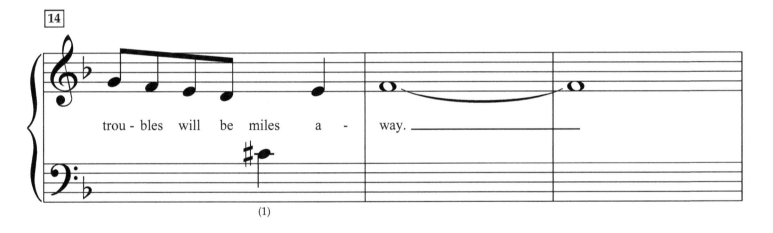

(1)

Here we are as in old-en days, hap-py gold-en days of

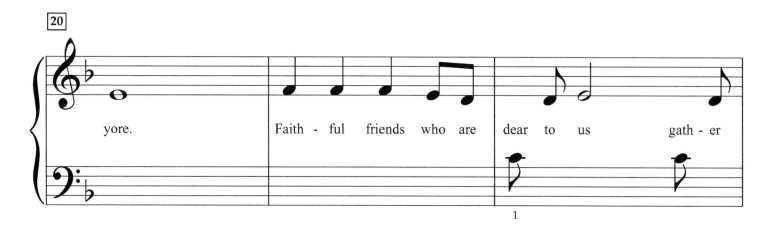

yore. Faith - ful friends who are dear to us gath - er

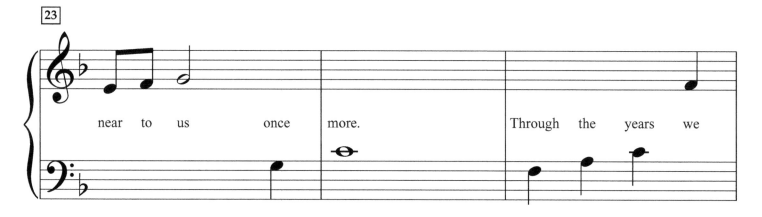

near to us once more. Through the years we

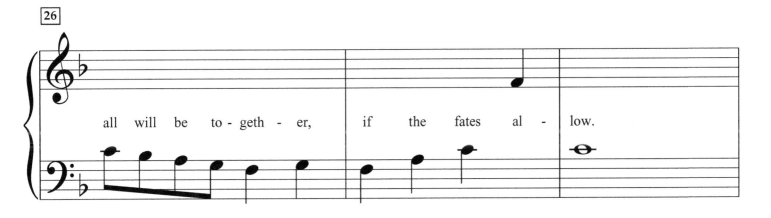

all will be to - geth - er, if the fates al - low.

Hang a shin - ing star up - on the high - est bough, _____ and

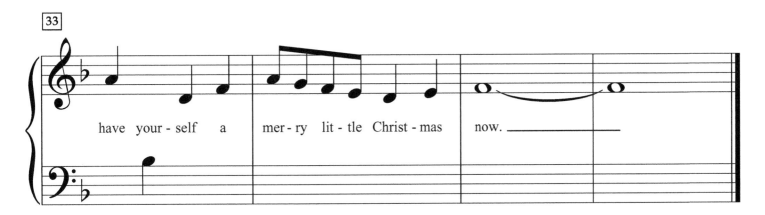

have your - self a mer - ry lit - tle Christ - mas now. _____

I Wonder as I Wander

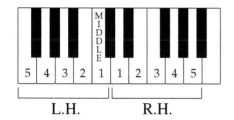

By John Jacob Niles

Moderately slow, with expression

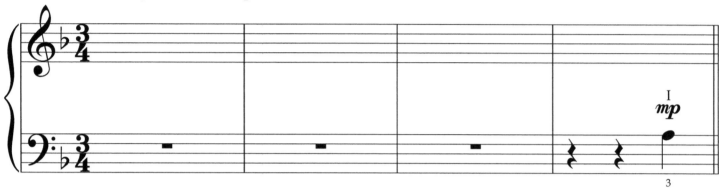

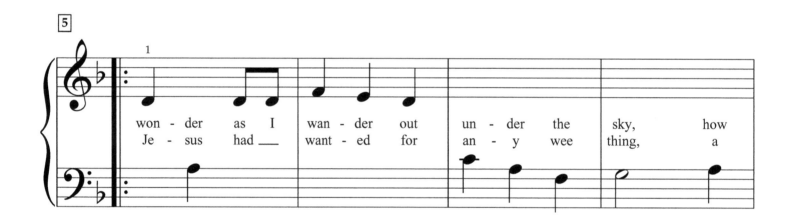

wonder as I wan-der out un-der the sky, how a
Je-sus had ___ want-ed for an-y wee thing, how a

Duet Part (Student plays one octave higher than written.)
Moderately slow, with expression

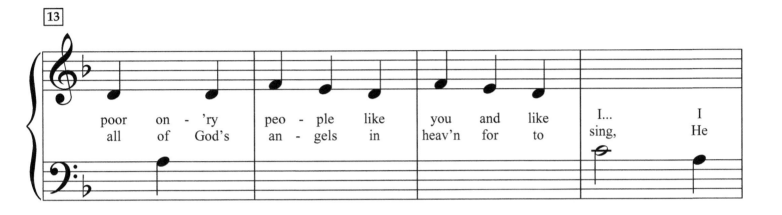

19

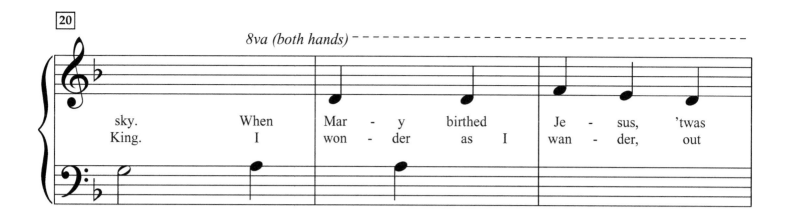

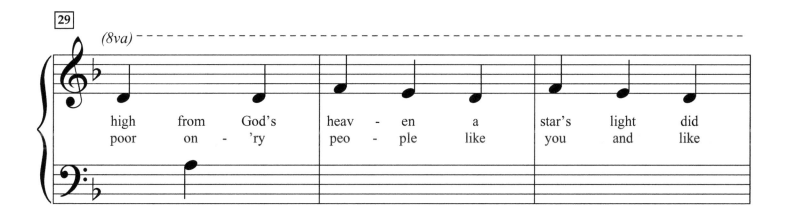

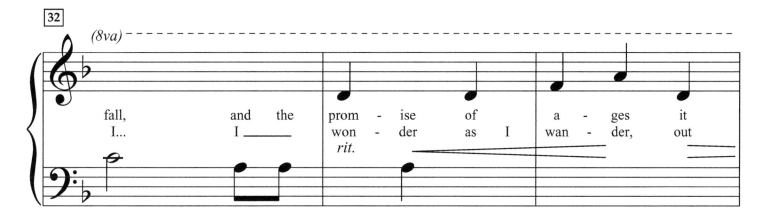

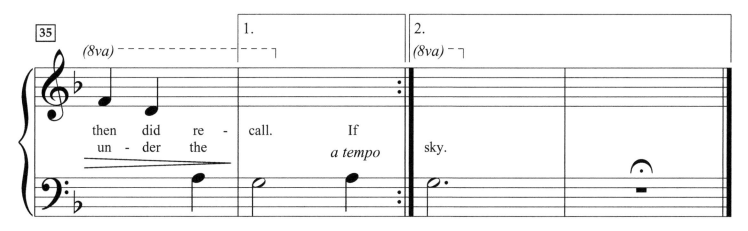

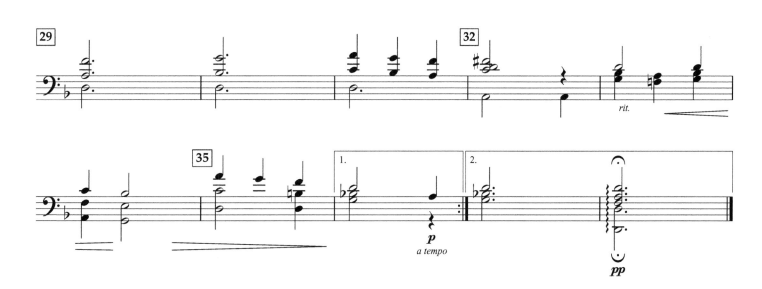

Jingle Bell Rock

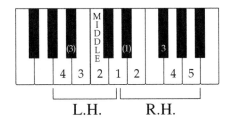

Words and Music by Joe Beal
and Jim Boothe

Duet Part (Student plays one octave higher than written.)

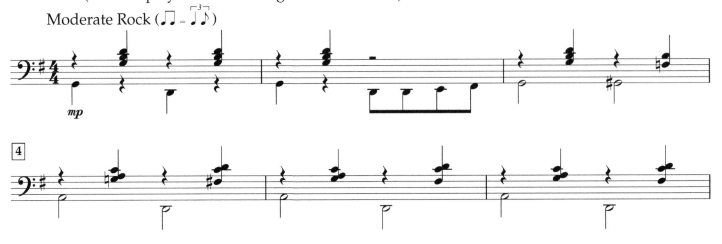

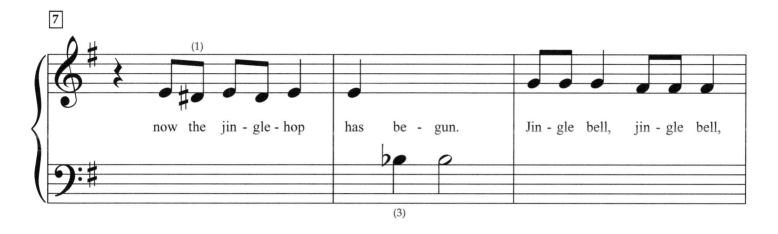

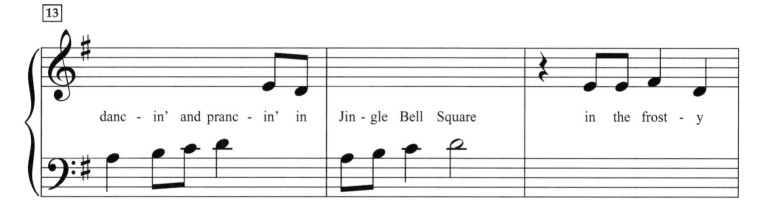

air. What a bright time, it's the right time to

rock the night a - way. Jin - gle bell time is a swell time

to go glid - in' in a one - horse sleigh. Gid - dy - ap, jin - gle horse,

pick up your feet,   jin-gle a - round the   clock.   Mix and min-gle in a

jin - gl - in'   beat.   That's the jin - gle bell   rock.

that's the jin - gle bell,   that's the jin - gle bell   rock.

Rockin' Around the Christmas Tree

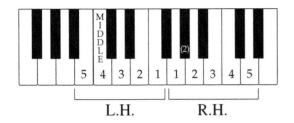

Music and Lyrics by
Johnny Marks

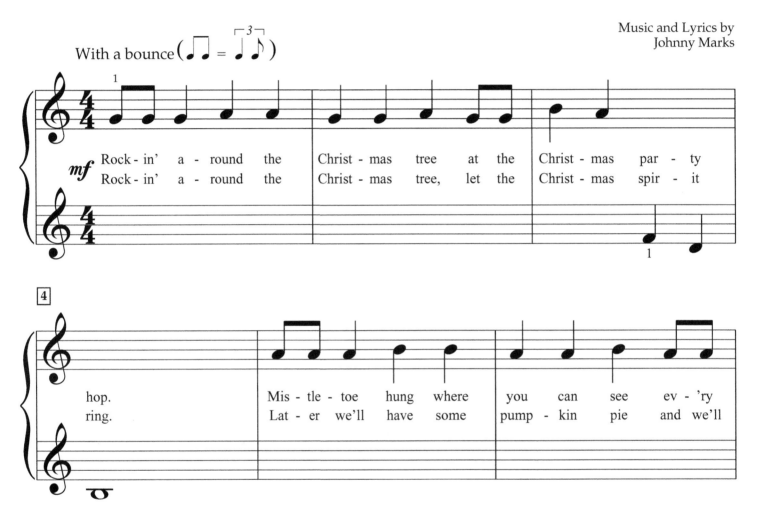

Duet Part (Student plays as written.)

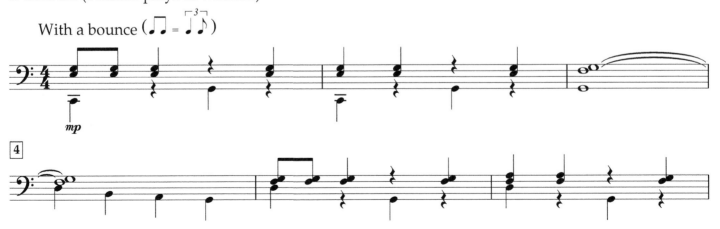

Mary, Did You Know?

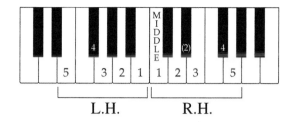

Words and Music by Mark Lowry
and Buddy Greene

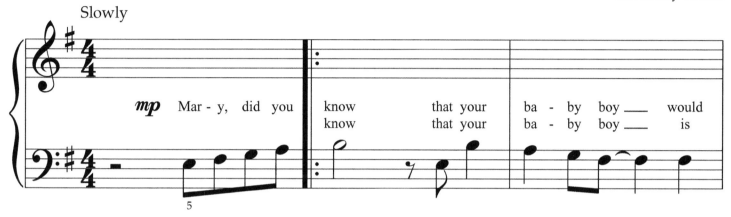

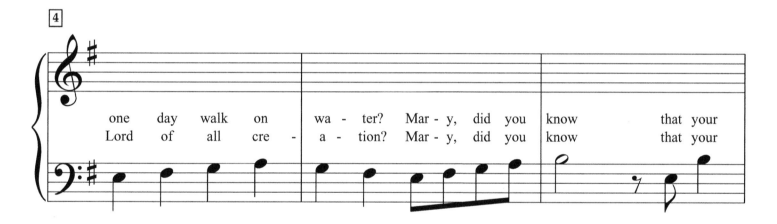

Duet Part (Student plays one octave higher than written.)

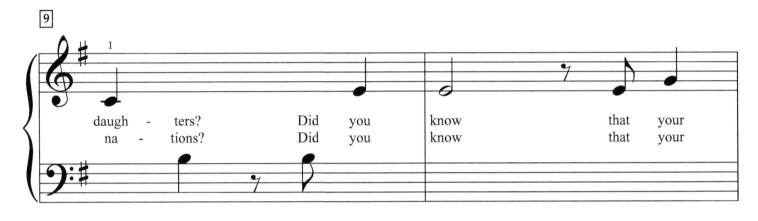

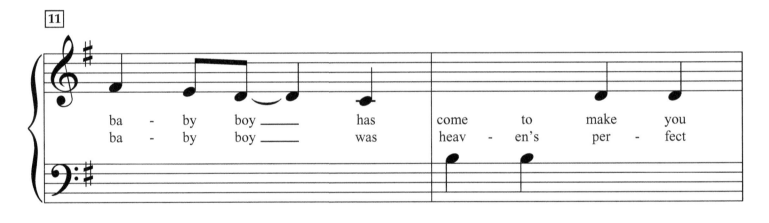

Sleigh Ride

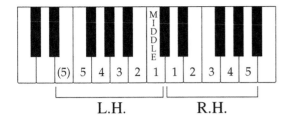

Music by Leroy Anderson
Words by Mitchell Parish

Briskly

mf Just hear those sleigh bells jin - gle - ing ring - ting - tin - gle - ing,
Out - side the snow is fall - ing and friends are call - ing, "Yoo

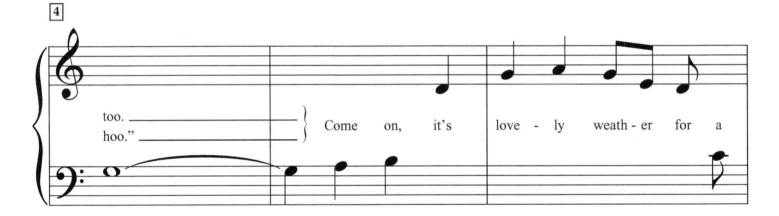

too. ____ Come on, it's love - ly weath - er for a
hoo." ____

Duet Part (Student plays one octave higher than written.)

Briskly

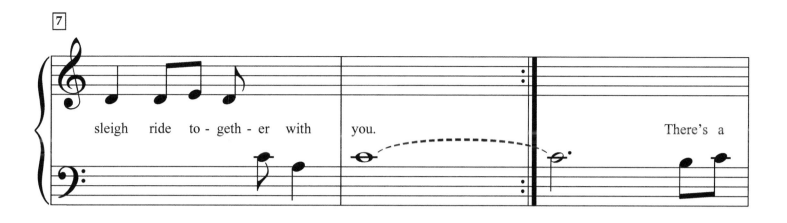

sleigh ride to - geth - er with you. There's a

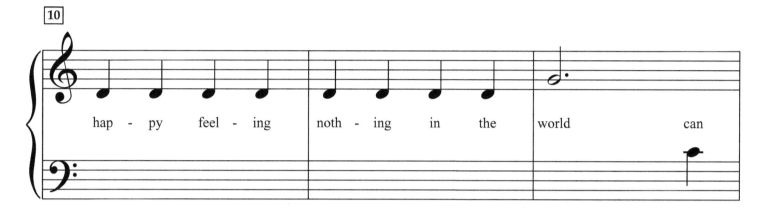

hap - py feel - ing noth - ing in the world can

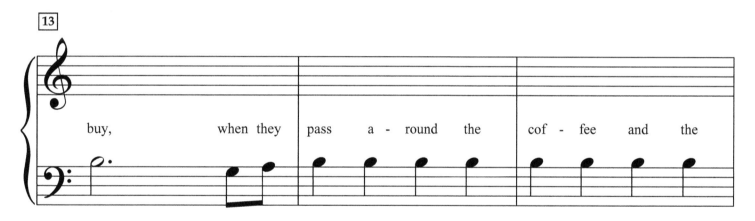

buy, when they pass a - round the cof - fee and the

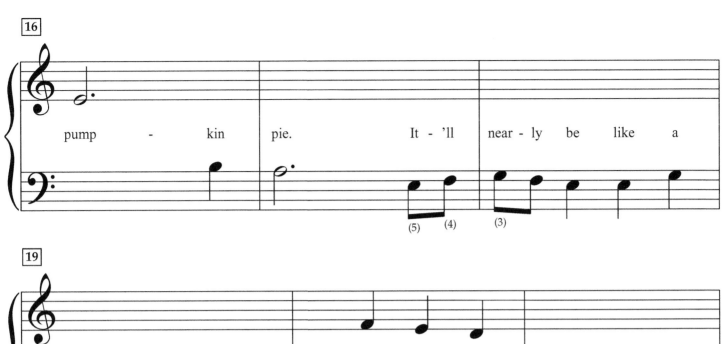

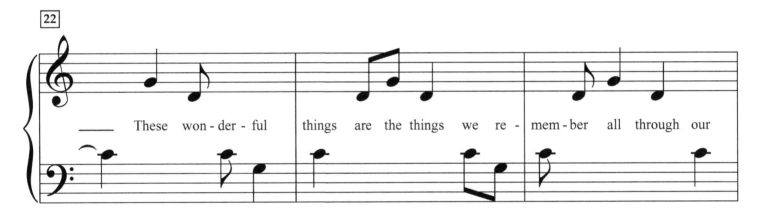

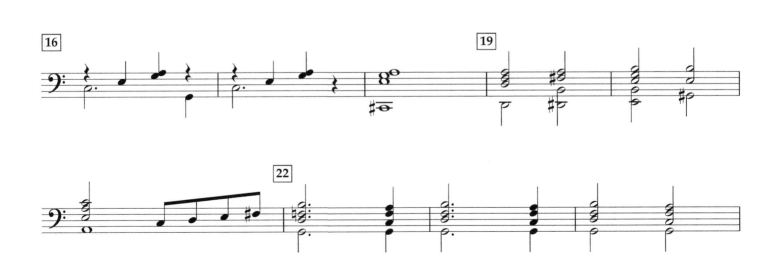

Wonderful Christmastime

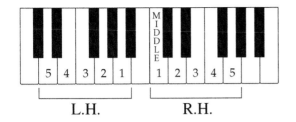

Words and Music by
Paul McCartney

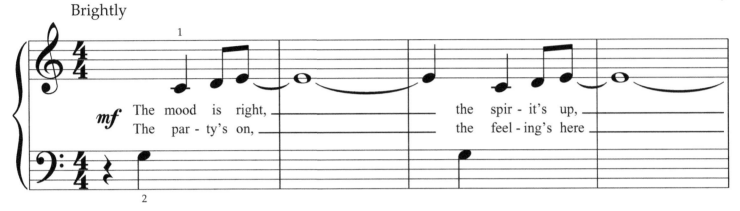

Brightly

The mood is right,   the spir - it's up,
The par - ty's on,   the feel - ing's here

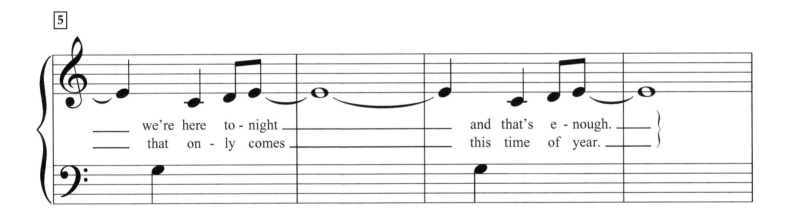

___ we're here to-night ___ and that's e - nough. ___
___ that on - ly comes ___ this time of year. ___

Duet Part (Student plays one octave higher than written.)

Brightly

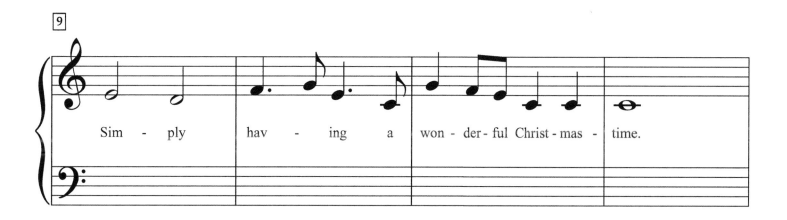

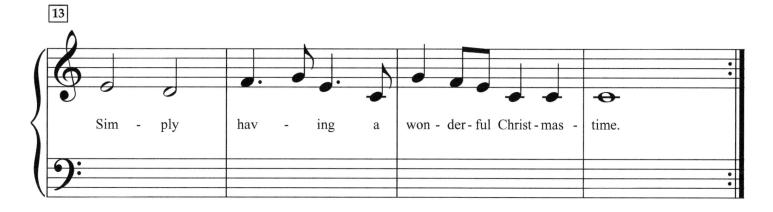

PLAYING PIANO HAS NEVER BEEN EASIER!

5-Finger Piano Collections from Hal Leonard

BEATLES! BEATLES!

8 classics, including: A Hard Day's Night • Hey Jude • Love Me Do • P.S. I Love You • Ticket to Ride • Twist and Shout • Yellow Submarine • Yesterday.
00292061...$8.99

CHILDREN'S TV FAVORITES
Themes from 8 Hit Shows

Five-finger arrangements of the themes for: Barney • Bob the Builder • Thomas the Tank Engine • Dragon Tales • PB&J Otter • SpongeBob SquarePants • Rugrats • Dora the Explorer.
00311208...$7.95

CHURCH SONGS FOR KIDS

Features five-finger arrangements of 15 sacred favorites, including: Amazing Grace • The B-I-B-L-E • Down in My Heart • Fairest Lord Jesus • Hallelu, Hallelujah! • I'm in the Lord's Army • Jesus Loves Me • Kum Ba Yah • My God Is So Great, So Strong and So Mighty • Oh, How I Love Jesus • Praise Him, All Ye Little Children • Zacchaeus • and more.
00310613...$8.99

CLASSICAL FAVORITES – 2ND EDITION

Includes 12 beloved classical pieces from Bach, Bizet, Haydn, Grieg and other great composers: Bridal Chorus • Hallelujah! • He Shall Feed His Flock • Largo • Minuet in G • Morning • Rondeau • Surprise Symphony • To a Wild Rose • Toreador Song.
00310611...$8.99

DISNEY MOVIE FUN

8 classics, including: Beauty and the Beast • When You Wish Upon a Star • Whistle While You Work • and more.
00292067...$8.99

DISNEY TUNES

Includes: Can You Feel the Love Tonight? • Chim Chim Cher-ee • Go the Distance • It's a Small World • Supercalifragilisticexpialidocious • Under the Sea • You've Got a Friend in Me • Zero to Hero.
00310375...$8.99

SELECTIONS FROM DISNEY'S PRINCESS COLLECTION VOL. 1

7 songs sung by Disney heroines – with a full-color illustration of each! Includes: Colors of the Wind • A Dream Is a Wish Your Heart Makes • I Wonder • Just Around the Riverbend • Part of Your World • Something There • A Whole New World.
00310847 ....$8.99

EENSY WEENSY SPIDER & OTHER NURSERY RHYME FAVORITES

Includes 11 rhyming tunes kids love: Hickory Dickory Dock • Humpty Dumpty • Hush, Little Baby • Jack and Jill • Little Jack Horner • Mary Had a Little Lamb • Peter, Peter Pumpkin Eater • Pop Goes the Weasel • Tom, Tom, the Piper's Son • more.
00310465...$7.95

FIRST POP SONGS

Eight timeless pop classics are presented here in accessible arrangements: Candle in the Wind • Lean on Me • Moon River • Piano Man • Tears in Heaven • Unchained Melody • What a Wonderful World • Yellow Submarine.
00123296...$8.99

FROZEN
Music from the Motion Picture

Seven popular songs from *Frozen* are featured in single-note melody lines that stay in one position in this songbook. Songs include: Do You Want to Build a Snowman? • Fixer Upper • For the First Time in Forever • In Summer • Let It Go • Love Is an Open Door • Reindeer(s) Are Better Than People. Includes lyrics and beautifully-written accompaniments.
00130374...$10.99

MODERN MOVIE FAVORITES

Eight modern movie songs including lyrics: Can't Stop the Feeling • City of Stars • Evermore • Everything Is Awesome (Awesome Remixx!!!) • How Far I'll Go • Spirit in the Sky • Try Everything • Unforgettable.
00242674...$9.99

POP HITS FOR FIVE-FINGER PIANO

8 hot hits that even beginners can play, including: Cups (When I'm Gone) • Home • I Won't Give Up • Love Story • Next to Me • Skyfall • What Makes You Beautiful • When I Was Your Man. These books also include optional duet parts for a teacher or parent to play that makes the student sound like a pro!
00123295...$9.99

THE SOUND OF MUSIC

8 big-note arrangements of popular songs from this perennial favorite musical, including: Climb Ev'ry Mountain • Do-Re-Mi • Edelweiss • The Lonely Goatherd • My Favorite Things • Sixteen Going on Seventeen • So Long, Farewell • The Sound of Music.
00310249...$10.99

SELECTIONS FROM *STAR WARS*
arr. Robert Schultz

Based on the fantastic series of *Star Wars* movies, these songs were carefully selected and arranged by Robert Schultz at the five finger level. Included in the folio are: Anakin's Theme • Augie's Great Municipal Band • Cantina Band • Duel of the Fates • The Imperial March • Luke and Leia • Princess Leia's Theme • Star Wars (Main Title) • Yoda's Theme.
00321903...$9.99

HAL•LEONARD®

www.halleonard.com

Disney Characters and Artwork TM & © 2018 Disney

Prices, contents and availability subject to change without notice.

Big Fun with Big-Note Piano Books!

These songbooks feature exciting easy arrangements for beginning piano students.

Beatles' Best

27 classics for beginners to enjoy, including: Can't Buy Me Love • Eleanor Rigby • Hey Jude • Michelle • Here, There and Everywhere • When I'm Sixty-Four • Yesterday • and more.
00222561..$14.99

The Best Songs Ever

70 favorites, featuring: Body and Soul • Crazy • Edelweiss • Fly Me to the Moon • Georgia on My Mind • Imagine • The Lady Is a Tramp • Memory • A String of Pearls • Tears in Heaven • Unforgettable • You Are So Beautiful • and more.
00310425..$19.95

Chart Hits of 2018-2019

15 of today's biggest hits. Songs include: Eastside (benny blanco with Halsey & Khalid) • High Hopes (Panic! At the Disco) • Sunflower (Post Malone & Swae Lee) • Without Me (Halsey) • and more.
00290100..$14.99

Children's Favorite Movie Songs

arranged by Phillip Keveren
16 favorites from films, including: The Bare Necessities • Beauty and the Beast • Can You Feel the Love Tonight • Do-Re-Mi • The Rainbow Connection • Tomorrow • Zip-A-Dee-Doo-Dah • and more.
00310838..$12.99

Disney Big-Note Collection

Over 40 Disney favorites, including: Circle of Life • Colors of the Wind • Hakuna Matata • It's a Small World • Under the Sea • A Whole New World • Winnie the Pooh • Zip-A-Dee-Doo-Dah • and more.
00316056..$19.99

Favorite Children's Songs

arranged by Bill Boyd
29 easy arrangements of songs to play and sing with children: Peter Cottontail • I Whistle a Happy Tune • It's a Small World • On the Good Ship Lollipop • The Rainbow Connection • and more!
00240251..$12.99

Favorite TV Themes

22 themes from the small screen, including: Addams Family Theme • Happy Days • Jeopardy Theme • Mission: Impossible Theme • Price Is Right (Opening Theme) • Sesame Street Theme • Won't You Be My Neighbor? • and more.
00294318..$10.99

Frozen

9 songs from this hit Disney film, plus full-color illustrations from the movie. Songs include the standout single "Let It Go", plus: Do You Want to Build a Snowman? • For the First Time in Forever • Reindeer(s) Are Better Than People • and more.
00126105..$12.99

The Great Big Book of Children's Songs – 2nd Edition

66 super tunes that kids adore, includes: Circle of Life • Edelweiss • If I Only Had a Brain • Over the Rainbow • Puff the Magic Dragon • Rubber Duckie • Sing • This Land Is Your Land • Under the Sea • and dozens more!
00119364..$17.99

Happy Birthday to You and Other Great Songs for Big-Note Piano

16 essential favorites, including: Chitty Chitty Bang Bang • Good Night • Happy Birthday to You • Heart and Soul • Over the Rainbow • Sing • This Land Is Your Land • and more.
00119636..$9.99

Modern Movie Favorites

Beginning pianists will love to play the 18 familiar movie hits in this collection, including: The Bare Necessities • Can't Stop the Feeling • City of Stars • How Far I'll Go • In Summer • Rey's Theme • Something Wild • and more.
00241880..$14.99

Pride & Prejudice

Music from the Motion Picture Soundtrack
12 piano pieces from the 2006 Oscar-nominated film: Another Dance • Darcy's Letter • Georgiana • Leaving Netherfield • Liz on Top of the World • Meryton Townhall • The Secret Life of Daydreams • Stars and Butterflies • and more.
00316125..$12.99

Songs of Peace, Hope and Love

30 inspirational and motivational songs, including: Bridge over Troubled Water • The Climb • Hallelujah • Over the Rainbow • Put a Little Love in Your Heart • What a Wonderful World • You Raise Me Up • and more.
00119634..$12.99

Star Wars

13 Selections from a Galaxy Far, Far Away
A baker's dozen of *Star Wars* selections by John Williams arranged by Phillip Keveren, include: Across the Stars (Love Theme from *Star Wars*) • The Imperial March (Darth Vader's Theme) • Luke and Leia • Rey's Theme • Star Wars (Main Theme) • and more.
00277371..$16.99

Today's Pop Hits – 3rd Edition

A great collection of current pop hits that even developing piano players will be able to enjoy. 15 songs with lyrics, including: All of Me • Happy • Hello • Pompeii • Radioactive • Roar • Shake It Off • Stay with Me • Story of My Life • and more.
00160577 ....$14.99

Top Hits of 2019

17 of the year's best are included in this collection for easy to read big note piano with lyrics: Gloria • I Don't Care • Lo/Hi • ME! • Old Town Road (Remix) • Senorita • Someone You Loved • Sucker • and more.
00302427..$14.99

The Big-Note Worship Book – 2nd Edition

20 selections for budding pianists looking to play their favorite worship songs: Everlasting God • Holy Is the Lord • In Christ Alone • Revelation Song • 10,000 Reasons (Bless the Lord) • Your Grace Is Enough • and more.
00267812..$12.99

HAL•LEONARD®

Complete song lists online at
www.halleonard.com